# A BUSINESS APPROACH TO KALE FARMING

I0427358

## Complete Entrepreneurial Step By Step Guide To Kale Garden From Scratch

## ZHURI HART

# DISCLAIMER

This book is intended to provide general information and insights on adopting a business approach to farming. The content within is based on the author's knowledge and experiences up to the date of publication. It is essential to recognize that the field of agriculture is dynamic, influenced by various factors such as market conditions, climate, and regulatory changes.

Readers are advised to conduct thorough research, seek professional advice, and consider their unique circumstances before implementing any strategies or practices discussed in this book. The author and publisher disclaim any responsibility for the accuracy, completeness, or suitability of the information provided. The book is not a substitute for professional advice, and the author and publisher shall not be liable for any damages or losses arising from the use or reliance on the information presented herein.

Individual results may vary, and success in farming enterprises is contingent upon numerous variables. The author encourages readers to consult with relevant experts, agricultural extension services, and legal or financial professionals to tailor strategies to their specific needs and local conditions.

This book is not intended to be a comprehensive guide to all aspects of farming, and readers should exercise their judgment and discretion in applying the principles discussed. The author and publisher do not endorse any specific products, services, or companies mentioned in this book unless explicitly stated.

By reading this book, the reader acknowledges and accepts the inherent uncertainties in agricultural endeavors and agrees to use the information at their own risk.

# TABLE OF CONTENTS

## ABOUT THE BOOK

A valuable resource for anyone interested in starting a kale farming business is the book "A Business Approach to Kale Farming." The thorough information is intended to provide readers with the know-how and abilities required to start and run a profitable kale farm. By explaining the history of kale farming, outlining the book's goals, defining its scope, identifying the target audience, and emphasizing the main advantages of kale farming, the introduction section lays a strong foundation.

In-depth information about kale farming, including the different types and traits of the plant, soil, and climate needs, and how a kale farm should be planned and designed. It also lists the tools and materials required, guaranteeing a realistic approach to farm setup.

The book discusses market research and demand analysis, is a crucial part of the book. The information provided to readers helps them with target market identification, trend research, understanding customer preferences, competitor analysis, and demand forecasting. The strategic basis for determining the market presence and profitability of a kale farm is given in this section.

The book walk readers through the process of developing a strong business plan, putting into practice efficient farming methods and strategies, and investigating organic and sustainable kale farming practices. The focus on budgeting and financial management guarantees that readers comprehend the financial aspects of kale growing and can make profitable judgments.

The construction of a brand identity, successful marketing tactics, digital marketing, and cultivating client connections are all covered in detail on marketing and branding. The book also discusses supply chain and distribution issues. It offers guidance on selecting distribution channels, organizing logistics for transportation, and preserving freshness and quality.

The book delves into legal and regulatory aspects, encompassing licenses and permissions, adhering to environmental guidelines, managing risks, and agricultural standards. By ensuring that readers are knowledgeable about the laws about kale cultivation, this section helps to reduce any potential concerns.

"A Business Approach to Kale Farming" is an essential tool for would-be kale farmers as it provides a thorough and organized overview of starting and running a profitable kale farm. This book is a vital resource for anyone hoping to succeed in the kale farming sector because it takes a systematic approach to every facet, from market research to legal issues.

# CHAPTER ONE

## KALE FARMING INTRODUCTION

### PRINCIPAL ADVANTAGES OF GROWING KALE

Because of the many health advantages and culinary diversity of kale, kale farming has been increasingly popular in recent years. This leafy green vegetable, which belongs to the Brassica oleracea family, is being cultivated and consumed more widely because it has become a staple in many diets around the world.

This in-depth summary will cover the main advantages of kale farming, delve into the nuances of understanding kale farming, look at the different varieties and traits of the kale plant, talk about the important factors related to soil requirements and climate, and offer tips for organizing and creating a productive kale farm. We will also discuss the essential tools and materials that are essential to the productive production of kale.

# PRIMARY ADVANTAGES OF GROWING KALE

The many health advantages of kale are a major factor in the growth of this leafy green's cultivation. Vitamins A, C, and K are among the many nutrients found in kale, along with minerals like calcium and iron. Its strong antioxidant concentration has been connected to several health advantages, including heart health and inflammation reduction.

In addition, kale is a high-fiber, low-calorie meal, which makes it a great option for anyone looking to control their weight and improve their digestion. Growing consumer knowledge of the benefits of eating a diet high in nutrients has led to a rise in the demand for kale, which is now a product that farmers can profit from.

## KNOWING HOW TO FARM KALE

A thorough understanding of the life cycle, development patterns, and ideal growing techniques are essential for successful kale farming. Farmers need to be knowledgeable about the several stages of kale production, from seed germination to harvesting. This includes understanding crop rotation techniques, optimum methods for soil enrichment, and managing pests and diseases. Additionally, a successful kale farming endeavor requires an awareness of consumer tastes and market dynamics.

## THE DIFFERENT TYPES OF KALE AND THEIR FEATURES

There are numerous types of kale, and each has a distinct mix of qualities, flavors, and textures. Lacinato, or dinosaur, kale, Red Russian kale, and curly kale are common varieties. Farmers need to choose carefully which types to plant to meet market demands and their special purposes. Farmers can increase the variety of products they plant and reach a wider market by learning about the growth patterns, color differences, and flavor characteristics of many varieties of kale.

## CONDITIONS OF THE SOIL AND CLIMATE

Although kale is a resilient plant that can grow in a variety of conditions, knowing the precise needs is essential for the best results. Even though kale is known for its capacity to withstand cold, it is still important to take temperature, sunlight, and water availability into account. In a similar vein, different varieties of kale could favor different types of soil, thus knowing the pH, nutrient content, and makeup of the soil is important. Farmers may maximize output and generate high-quality crops by adjusting the growing conditions to suit the needs of kale.

## ORGANIZING AND CREATING A KALE FARM

Effective design and planning are essential components of a profitable kale farming business. A few of the things that farmers need to think about are crop rotation plans, irrigation systems, and field structure. The long-term sustainability of the kale farm can also be enhanced by implementing environmentally friendly agricultural methods. A thorough planning step is necessary to ensure that important factors like sufficient plant spacing, appropriate row orientation, and effective use of the available land are taken into account.

## TOOLS AND MATERIALS

A kale farm must have the appropriate equipment and supplies to maximize output and reduce manual work. Farmers need to make investments in machinery and technology that match the size of their enterprise, from irrigation systems to planting equipment. Furthermore, the key to a great kale crop is having access to high-quality seeds, fertilizers, and insect control techniques. A well-equipped kale farm guarantees a smooth and effective production process from planting to harvesting.

In summary, kale farming offers a variety of advantages to growers and customers alike, from financial stability to health benefits.

This introduction offers an overview of the diverse realm of kale cultivation, stressing the significance of comprehending the plant, choosing suitable cultivars, taking soil and climate conditions into account, and putting good planning and design techniques into practice. We will learn about the complexities that contribute to the success of this growingly popular agricultural effort as we delve deeper into the subtleties of kale cultivation.

# CHAPTER TWO

## DEMAND ANALYSIS AND MARKET RESEARCH

### FINDING THE RIGHT TARGET MARKETS

One of the most important steps in the market research and demand analysis process is identifying target markets. It entails a thorough investigation of the characteristics, psychographics, and behavior of prospective clients who are most likely to buy a specific good or service.

Businesses can concentrate their marketing efforts and resources on the market segments with the highest potential for success thanks to this technique. Companies can identify the unique traits and requirements of their target market using techniques like surveys, interviews, and data analysis, which enables them to develop more focused and successful marketing campaigns.

# EXAMINING MARKET PATTERNS

Market trends have a significant influence on how businesses formulate their plans and make decisions. A comprehensive examination of market trends entails monitoring trends, changes, and advancements that impact consumer conduct, technological advancements, and the general dynamics of the industry. Businesses can modify their goods and services to satisfy changing customer needs and maintain their competitiveness in the market by keeping up with current developments. This could involve keeping an eye on new developments in technology, cultural trends, or legislative frameworks to provide insightful information that businesses can use to strategically position themselves within their particular industries.

## RECOGNIZING CUSTOMER PREFERENCES

Demand analysis and market research are successful when they are based on an understanding of consumer preferences. It entails exploring the elements—such as lifestyle choices, societal influences, and personal preferences—that affect consumers' purchase decisions. Through focus groups, polls, and social media monitoring, businesses can obtain significant insights into the factors that influence consumer choices. By better-aligning goods and services with consumer preferences, this information can be leveraged to improve customer happiness and loyalty.

## ANALYSIS OF COMPETITORS

An essential component of market research is competitor analysis, which gives companies knowledge about the tactics, advantages, and disadvantages of their rivals. Firms can find chances for difference and competitive advantage by closely analyzing the products, pricing policies, marketing tactics, and consumer feedback of rivals. Businesses may improve their strategies, take advantage of market gaps, and create distinctive value propositions that differentiate them from competitors by having a thorough understanding of the competitive landscape.

# PREDICTING THE DEMAND

Demand forecasting helps organizations anticipate future market needs and allocate resources appropriately. It is a crucial part of strategic planning. Analyzing previous sales data, industry trends, and outside variables that can affect demand are all part of this process. Precise demand projections facilitate inventory control, production scheduling, and corporate strategy in general. By taking a proactive stance, businesses may react quickly to shifting market conditions, avoid shortages or overstock, and make sure they effectively meet client demand. Demand forecasting is also essential for spotting expansion prospects and fine-tuning price plans in response to expected changes in the market.

# CHAPTER THREE

## FORMULATING A BUSINESS STRATEGY

### EXECUTIVE SYNOPSIS

The executive summary provides a succinct, all-inclusive synopsis of the main components of the organization clearly and concisely. It summarizes the goals, competitive advantages, market niche, and financial predictions of the business. This part is essential because it gives stakeholders and possible investors a brief overview of the company model and its chances of success.

### OVERVIEW OF THE COMPANY

The company overview goes into great depth about the specifics of the company, including its location, history, legal structure, and important operational details. The purpose of this part is to give a contextual understanding of the establishment and development of the firm.

It also highlights the strengths that contribute to the success of the organization by introducing key team members and their duties.

## GOALS AND OBJECTIVES

Foundational components that express the goal and direction of the company are the mission and vision statements. The mission statement describes the primary rationale for the company's existence as well as its key principles and the benefits it hopes to bring to its constituents. On the other hand, the vision statement provides a forward-looking viewpoint by describing the long-term objectives and aspirations that the company hopes to accomplish.

## OBJECTIVES AND GOALS

The precise, quantifiable benchmarks that a firm seeks to achieve within a specified term are outlined in its goals and objectives. These objectives provide doable milestones that complement the company's overarching mission and vision, acting as a guide for its expansion and prosperity. Having clearly defined goals and objectives makes it easier to concentrate efforts, allocate resources wisely, and assess the company's development over time.

## SWOT EVALUATION

A strategic tool called the SWOT analysis evaluates the company's external opportunities and market threats in addition to its internal strengths and weaknesses. The development of a comprehensive awareness of the corporate environment made possible by this research is crucial for strategic planning and efficient decision-making.

The SWOT analysis provides a basis for developing plans that build on the company's strengths and solve its weaknesses by recognizing internal capabilities and external factors that may have an impact on the operation.

## BUDGETARY ESTIMATES

A company's financial performance over a given period is projected in depth using financial predictions. Cash flow statements, balance sheets, and income statements are usually included in this part. These forecasts are used by stakeholders and investors to evaluate the company's growth prospects and financial stability. Financial projections must be grounded in reasonable assumptions and current market conditions to show a thorough comprehension of the financial dynamics of the company.

# CHAPTER FOUR

## TECHNIQUES AND PRACTICES IN FARMING

### SELECTION AND GERMINATION OF SEEDS

A vital first step in effective agricultural techniques is choosing the right seeds. A farmer's selection of seeds should take into consideration various elements, including soil type, climate, and crop requirements. Better germination rates and general crop health are ensured by premium seeds possessing favorable genetic characteristics. To increase productivity and resistance to pests and diseases, hybrid and genetically modified seeds are used in modern agricultural methods.

The process through which a seed develops into a new plant is called germination. Effective germination is essential for a robust beginning to the crop cycle. Farmers use a variety of strategies, such as ideal moisture and temperature levels, to encourage germination.

During the germination stage, seed treatments with fungicides and insecticides can also be used to shield young plants from possible dangers.

## HANDLING CROPS AND PLANTING

Planting the seeds in the field comes next after they have germinated. Depending on the crop and regional agricultural practices, different planting methods exist. To ensure good crop development, planting depth, plant spacing, and soil preparation are essential. Utilizing equipment like planters or seed drills, farmers can attain planting consistency.

A variety of techniques are used in crop care to encourage healthy plant growth and development. Eliminating undesired plants that vie for nutrients and sunlight is imperative. Fertilization with appropriate nutrients enhances crop health, and farmers may employ organic or synthetic fertilizers based on soil nutrient analysis.

Monitoring for symptoms of pests and illnesses is especially vital during the growth season.

## IRRIGATION AND WATER MANAGEMENT

Efficient water management is crucial for sustainable farming methods. Depending on the temperature and soil conditions, farmers apply various irrigation techniques such as drip irrigation, sprinkler systems, or classic furrow irrigation.

Adequate water supply is essential for crop growth, and timing plays a crucial role in maximizing water use efficiency.

Water management also involves water conservation practices, such as rainwater harvesting and the use of moisture-retaining techniques like mulching. Proper drainage systems help prevent waterlogging, which can adversely affect root health and overall crop performance. Integrating technology, like soil moisture sensors, can aid farmers in making informed decisions about irrigation scheduling.

## PEST AND DISEASE CONTROL

Pest and disease control is a constant challenge for farmers. Integrated Pest Management (IPM) approaches are increasingly popular, focusing on a combination of biological, cultural, and chemical control methods. Biological control involves using natural predators or parasites to manage pest populations, while cultural practices may include crop rotation and selecting resistant crop varieties.

Chemical control, such as the use of pesticides, is a common method but requires careful consideration to minimize environmental impact and avoid resistance development. Regular monitoring of crops for signs of pests and diseases allows farmers to implement timely interventions and prevent widespread infestations.

## HARVESTING AND POST-HARVEST HANDLING

The culmination of the farming cycle is the harvest, a critical phase that directly influences the quality and yield of the final product. Harvesting techniques vary across crops, and factors such as maturity, weather conditions, and market demand influence the timing of harvest. Mechanical harvesters are often employed for large-scale operations, while smaller farms may rely on manual harvesting methods.

Post-harvest handling involves activities that preserve the quality of the harvested crop until it reaches consumers. Proper storage, transportation, and processing are essential components of post-harvest management. Farmers use techniques such as drying, curing, and refrigeration to prevent spoilage and maintain the nutritional value of the produce. Implementing good post-harvest practices is crucial for reducing losses and ensuring a sustainable food supply chain.

# CHAPTER FIVE

## ORGANIC AND SUSTAINABLE KALE FARMING

### ADVANTAGES OF ECOLOGICAL AGRICULTURE

Growing kale sustainably and organically requires a comprehensive strategy that prioritizes long-term viability and environmental responsibility. The benefits that sustainable farming offers to the ecosystem are among its main advantages. Farming communities may preserve healthy and productive land for future generations by implementing measures that reduce soil degradation, conserve water, and foster biodiversity. Additionally, by using less artificial fertilizers and chemicals, sustainable farming lessens the environmental impact of conventional agriculture.

### CERTIFICATION FOR ORGANIC PRODUCTS

An essential component of organic and sustainable kale production is organic certification. Certification guarantees that farming techniques meet certain requirements that favor natural processes over artificial inputs. Strict inspections and adherence to regulations established by pertinent certifying authorities are frequently necessary for organic certification. Organic farmers are more credible in the market because consumers are starting to value products made without the use of toxic chemicals or genetically modified organisms.

## ENVIRONMENTALLY FRIENDLY METHODS

The foundation of organic and sustainable kale cultivation is eco-friendly methods. Crop rotation, cover crops, and integrated pest control are some of these techniques that improve soil health and reduce the need for chemical inputs. Furthermore, adding compost and organic fertilizers to the soil enriches it with vital elements, creating an environment that is rich in minerals and ideal for growing kale. Water conservation strategies, such as rainwater collection and drip irrigation, are essential for reducing water use and fostering effective resource management.

## PROMOTING ORGANIC KALE

Promoting organic kale entails connecting with customers who care about the environment and raising awareness of the advantages of buying organic vegetables. Emphasizing the lack of artificial fertilizers and pesticides, together with the use of sustainable farming methods, can be important selling points. Making use of clear labeling and eco-friendly packaging also appeals to customers who are looking to make ecologically beneficial decisions. Farmers can work with grocery stores that promote organic and sustainable products, engage in farmers' markets, or investigate joint ventures with nearby markets. Social media and digital marketing can be effective strategies for highlighting the farm's dedication to organic and sustainable farming methods and drawing in customers who respect eco-friendly products.

Organic and sustainable kale growing has many advantages, including satisfying consumer demand for organic food and protecting the environment and soil health. While eco-friendly methods contribute to the operation's overall sustainability, organic certification lends legitimacy to farming practices. To build a relationship between the farm and ethical customers, marketing organic kale entails explaining to consumers the advantages of sustainable methods that are important to them.

# CHAPTER SIX

## BUDGETING AND FINANCIAL MANAGEMENT

Any effective financial strategy, whether for a corporation or a person, must include budgeting and money management. Long-term sustainability and performance depend on having a solid understanding of fundamental ideas including initial investment, operating costs, revenue creation, profitability analysis, and putting good financial management advice into practice.

### FIRST INVESTMENT

The money needed to launch a new venture or fund a firm is known as the initial investment. This covers charges for things like purchasing equipment, establishing infrastructure, and paying for startup operational expenses. A venture's early stages may face financial difficulties if undercapitalization is not avoided, which makes it crucial to carefully assess the first investment. To determine the feasibility and possible profitability of the first investment, a return on investment (ROI) analysis is essential.

## OPERATIONAL COSTS

These are the daily expenses that come with operating a firm. Rent, utilities, salaries, raw materials, and other variable expenditures are included in this. Sustaining profitability requires effective management of operating costs. Finding opportunities for cost savings without sacrificing the caliber of the goods or services can be accomplished by routinely analyzing and optimizing these costs. Keeping an eye on operating expenses facilitates improved financial planning and aids in responding to shifting market dynamics.

The process of generating income via the selling of products or services is known as revenue creation.

Sustainable growth requires diversifying sources of income and comprehending consumer demand for goods and services. Companies should always be looking for ways to grow their clientele, launch new goods, or penetrate untapped areas. Increasing revenue generation requires effective marketing and customer relationship management.

Analysis of a company's financial performance to ascertain its potential for long-term profit-making is known as profitability analysis. It entails evaluating elements like return on investment, net profit margin, and gross profit margin. Determining key performance indicators (KPIs) and routinely examining financial accounts aid in comprehending the situation of the company as a whole. When it comes to making well-informed decisions and putting plans into action that support long-term success, profitability analysis is essential.

## FINANCIAL MANAGEMENT ADVICE

A stable and successful business is built on sound financial management. First and foremost, keeping track of income and expenses requires developing a thorough budget. Examining financial statements regularly facilitates trend recognition and decision-making. Keeping a cash reserve on hand is essential for unanticipated costs and economic downturns. Businesses could also look into ways to improve cash flow, like providing early payment discounts or negotiating advantageous terms for supplier payments.

Accounting software is one kind of financial management technology that can be used to automate procedures and get real-time data. Maintaining a healthy cash flow requires building a strong credit management system that includes tracking receivables and managing payables. Last but not least, consulting with financial professionals, such as accountants and financial planners, can offer insightful counsel and direction for making wise financial decisions.

# CHAPTER SEVEN

## PROMOTIONS AND LABELS

### ESTABLISHING A PERSONAL BRAND

Developing a distinctive and enduring brand identity is essential for making a lasting impression on consumers. It entails creating a coherent and unified collection of linguistic and visual components that encapsulate a brand's core values.

This consists of an eye-catching logo, a color scheme, appealing typography, and a brand voice those appeals to the intended market. Having a thorough understanding of the brand's values, mission, and intended emotions is essential for creating a successful brand identity.

Maintaining consistency throughout all touchpoints is essential to making sure that customers can quickly identify and relate to the brand.

## SUCCESSFUL MARKETING TECHNIQUES

Any firm that wants to succeed must have effective marketing tactics, which include a variety of actions meant to advertise goods and services to a certain market. A strong value offer, competitive analysis, and in-depth market research to comprehend customer wants and habits are all necessary components of a winning marketing plan. Reaching a varied audience requires utilizing a variety of traditional and digital media. To maximize the total approach, the plan should also take into account the marketing mix, which incorporates the four Ps: product, pricing, location, and promotion. As market conditions change over time, adaptability and flexibility become increasingly important.

# KALE FARMS' DIGITAL MARKETING STRATEGY

In the age of digital domination, companies like Kale Farms that want to increase their effect and reach must use digital marketing. Kale Farms might use email marketing, content marketing, social media marketing, and search engine optimization (SEO) in a comprehensive digital marketing plan. Brand visibility can be increased by using influencers, sharing recipes, and producing interesting material on the health advantages of kale. Furthermore, an e-commerce platform can expedite the buying procedure and give clients a practical means of accessing Kale Farms' items online.

## DEVELOPING CONNECTIONS WITH CUSTOMERS

Developing enduring relationships with clients is essential to the success of any organization. This entails bringing in new clients while also keeping hold of current ones by providing outstanding customer support and tailored experiences. Understanding the requirements and interests of customers requires effective communication. Building trust is facilitated by keeping things transparent and using customer input for ongoing development. Exclusive deals and loyalty schemes can encourage recurring business even more. Creating a brand community on social media or other platforms can improve the customer experience and boost a person's sense of belonging.

## SALES AND PROMOTIONS

Promoting goods and services well is crucial to boosting sales and building brand recognition. Reductions, time-limited offers, and package reductions are just a few of the ways that promotions can be offered. A well-implemented promotional plan complements the marketing objectives and overall brand identity. Contrarily, sales entail the process of turning prospective clients into real purchasers. Developing relationships, addressing client needs, and using compelling selling approaches are a few examples of sales strategy. Maintaining a fresh strategy that draws in new clients while preserving the loyalty of current ones is ensured by striking a balance between sales and promotions.

# CHAPTER EIGHT

## SUPPLY CHAIN AND DISTRIBUTION

### SELECTING CHANNELS OF DISTRIBUTION

Selecting distribution channels is a crucial choice for companies since it has an immediate effect on how goods are delivered to final customers. The process of choosing a distribution channel entails evaluating several variables, including the product's characteristics, the target market, and financial constraints.

Manufacturers can choose between indirect distribution methods, which use middlemen like wholesalers and retailers, and direct channels, which use their own sales force and resources.

The decision is frequently influenced by the company's resources, market penetration, and preferred degree of control over the distribution process.

## LOGISTICS AND TRANSPORTATION

As the lifeline connecting different sites in the network, logistics and transportation are essential to the distribution and supply chain. Effective transportation lowers expenses, guarantees on-time delivery, and improves the performance of the supply chain as a whole. Businesses need to carefully plan their transportation strategies, taking into account things like route optimization, technology integration for real-time tracking, and the mode of transportation (air, sea, rail, or road). Managing inventory, warehousing, and order fulfillment are all parts of logistics management, which is equally important when it comes to optimizing the efficiency of the supply chain.

## COLLABORATING WITH RESTAURANTS AND RETAILERS

A crucial component of distribution, particularly for consumer goods and food products, is collaborating with stores and eateries. Working with retailers entails getting to know their unique needs, settling on terms, and building trusting relationships. Retailers and manufacturers have a symbiotic connection in which both depend on the other to succeed. Partnering with restaurants in the food business involves additional issues such as supply chain transparency, menu integration, and meeting quality standards. Developing trusting connections with these middlemen is crucial to guaranteeing a smooth transition of goods from production to consumption.

## ENSURING QUALITY AND FRESHNESS

Freshness and quality control are crucial, especially in the food and pharmaceutical industries. It is a complex issue to maintain product integrity throughout the supply chain, requiring cautious handling, storage, and transportation. For example, cold chain logistics is essential to ensure that temperature-sensitive products reach consumers in excellent condition. Enforcing industry standards and conducting routine inspections are examples of quality control procedures that assist in maintaining a brand's reputation and building client trust. IoT sensors and blockchain are two examples of technological innovations that are being used more and more to track and monitor product conditions in real time, bringing transparency and accountability to the supply chain.

To sum up, supply chain management and distribution are complex processes that necessitate strategic decision-making at different phases. Parts of a successful supply chain include selecting the right routes for distribution, streamlining logistics and shipping, working successfully with merchants and eateries, and guaranteeing freshness and quality. Businesses that successfully manage these components will be in a better position to satisfy customer demands, cut expenses, and obtain a competitive advantage in the marketplace.

# CHAPTER NINE

## REGULATORY AND LEGAL ASPECTS

### LICENSES AND PERMITS

Especially in the agriculture industry, permits and licenses are essential to maintaining regulatory compliance and commercial operations. Starting and running a farm or agricultural business requires obtaining the required licenses and permissions. These licenses, which are usually issued by government organizations, are intended to control several different things, including the use of pesticides, land usage, water rights, and animal welfare.

Obtaining permissions may require proving that certain requirements are met, upholding environmental regulations, and guaranteeing the security of agricultural operations. Legal repercussions, such as penalties or the suspension of operations, may arise from failing to get the necessary permissions.

## OBSERVANCE OF AGRICULTURAL STANDARDS

Maintaining the integrity of the agricultural sector and guaranteeing the caliber and safety of agricultural output depends heavily on adherence to agricultural standards. A variety of rules and regulations about topics including food safety, animal welfare, and sustainable farming techniques are included in agricultural standards. Following these guidelines protects consumers' health and welfare and improves the standing of agricultural enterprises. Adherence to particular farming techniques, frequent inspections, and strict record-keeping are frequently necessary for compliance. Maintaining a competitive edge in the market and navigating the ever-changing environment of agricultural regulations require staying up to date with evolving standards.

## RULES REGARDING THE ENVIRONMENT

Environmental regulations are essential to agricultural firms operating responsibly and sustainably. These laws aim to lessen the negative effects that farming has on the environment by addressing issues including habitat destruction, water pollution, and soil erosion. Using ecologically friendly pesticides, conserving soil, and ethically handling waste are all possible ways to comply with environmental requirements. In addition to posing threats to the environment, breaking these standards may result in legal ramifications and harm the agriculture industry's reputation. Maintaining a positive relationship between agribusiness and the ecosystems it works in requires proactive involvement with environmental rules.

# HAZARD ASSESSMENT

An essential component of managing the inherent uncertainty in the agriculture industry is risk management. Risks faced by farmers and agricultural enterprises include weather-related difficulties, market volatility, and regulatory changes. Identifying possible risks, evaluating their implications, and creating plans to reduce or transfer them are all necessary steps in the implementation of efficient risk management techniques. Common risk management techniques include insurance, crop diversification, and the use of resilient farming practices. Agricultural enterprises may improve their resilience, continuity, and economic sustainability in an ever-changing regulatory and environmental setting by foreseeing and mitigating future issues.